RAVANA THE GREAT: KING OF LANKA

RAVANA THE GREAT: KING OF LANKA

M. S. PURNALINGAM PILLAI

GYAN

Published by

Gyan Publishing House
5, Ansari Road
Daryaganj, New Delhi-110002
Phone: 011-47034999, 9811692060
E-mail: books@gyanbooks.com

Distribution Network
gyanbooks.com
India, USA, Canada, UK, Australia, France

ISBN : 978-81-212-3937-0 (PB)
First Published, 1928

2nd Impression 2020

Printed at: Gyan Press, Delhi.

Ravana The Great: King of Lanka
Author: M. S. Purnalingam Pillai

Rāvana The Great:
KING OF LANKA

IN ELEVEN CHAPTERS,
WITH MAP AND APPENDIX

BY

M. S. PURNALINGAM PILLAI, B.A., L.T.,

Emeritus Professor of English, Bishop Heber College, Trichinopoly, and Author of Tamil India, Ten Tamil Saints, etc.

PUBLISHED BY

THE BIBLIOTHECA, MUNNIRPALLAM,
Tinnevelly District.

1928

Dedicated to

Tiruvalar

T. P. Ponnambalam Pillai Avl., M.R.A.S.

Retired Excise Commissioner,

Travancore, now residing at Sivasailam,

Alvarkurichi Post, Tinnevelly District,

As a token of the Author's regard and esteem for him

as a pioneer researcher in the epic of Ramayana

and vindicator of the greatness of Ravana, the illustrious King of Lanka.

CONTENTS.

FOREWORD.

The Cynical review of the ' Tamil India by the Reader of the Madras Mail under the glaring head-line *Tamilians* ! *Excelsior* ! has only confirmed the author's statements in his Foreword to that book. Everybody knows that the time has not arrived for writing a history of South India and that the materials available for it are not only not enough but scattered over a wide area. The 'Tamil India', which does not lay claim to much originality, has, as The Indian Daily Mail of Bombay has put it, attempted to bring the available materials together under certain heads with a view to facilitate the work of the future historian. The aerial car, or the aeroplane was unimaginable to the ordinary Britisher of some thirty years back though it had been known to the Tamil Indian in the form of ' mair-porri ' or the ' Peacock Engine and Pushpaka Vimanam or the Flowery Car twenty centuries ago. The live frog under the rock is a too commonillustration of the mysterious divine governance, among the Tamilians, though it might have come within the purview of a few earnest gelogists. Telepathy, Clairvoyance, Clairaudience, *et hoc genus omne* have in quite recent times claimed the serious thought and attention of the greatest scientists of the west. If the hasty Reader, who has professed himself to be a highly discerning critic and to be endowed with the indispensable technique of the proverbial Indian 'annam' or swan, should chance to come across this little book, he would certainly play to the gallery with the blazing head-line *Rakshas* ! *Excelsior* ! It is hard to expect that men who have moved in particular grooves for years will ever easily get out of them or that the deep-rooted prejudices consecrated by time and circumstances will die an easy death. The much-maligned Ravana of the earliest Aryan Chronicler and purana writer and of the thoughtless Dravidian echoer of subsequent times cannot have his merits and virtues duly recognised until English education, now pursued merely as bread-study, broadens and liberalises the cramped and idola-obsessed Indian mind and wipes out his slave mentality altogether. If this booklet will provoke thought on the subject, its author will feel amply repaid for his labours.

SOME OPINIONS.

ON TAMIL INDIA.

1. *The Hindu*, Nov. 2, 1927:—"....One cannot but admit that the book contains much original matter and embodies considerable research work.....The book is a primer fit to be placed in the hands of every one who would like to learn about the ancient Tamils, their characteristic qualities, their language and literature, their philosophy and religion, their social life, their commercial enterprises, their politics and modes of warfare, their knowledge of the arts and the sciences, and their education in general. As frontispiece we have three maps showing the Southern Continent and India as they were (1) before the Puranic deluge, (2) after the deluge, and (3) in the first century A. D."

2. *The Madras Mail*, Dec. 19, 1927:—"The author has done a great deal of reading and is conversant with many works in the field of his investigation."

3. *The Daily Indian Mail*, Dec. 4, 1927:—"....Mr. Purnalingam Pillai has in his book *Tamil India* put together a number of

ideas which may serve as notes for the future historian of the Tamil race....The author's knowledge of Tamil has enabled him to cull quotations from ancient Tamil authors about Tamil arts, sciences and philosophy."

4. *The United India and Indian States*, Jan. 14, 1928 :—"....Mr. Purnalingam Pillai shows, on the strength of reliable recorded evidence, the antiquity and the grandeur of the Tamilian Civilisation, greater and more ancient than the Babylonian or Egyptian or even the ancient Aryan culture of North India....It is a consolation to learn that, in the interchange of culture that makes the world's progress, 'Tamil India' has exerted a wide-spread and vital influence...."

5. *The Mysore Economic Journal* :—"....Mr. Purnalingam Pillai has at great pains done his mite to dispel the veil that shrouds the origin and antiquity of Tamil culture.... Tamil Language and Literature, Warfare, Polity, Medicine and Philosophy are some of the subjects which come under the author's observation and analysis........This book makes a bold effort to elucidate the tangled skein of ancient Tamil culture....Readers would do well to buy this book and know something of ancient Tamilians quite profitably...."

6. *The Hon'ble P. Ramanathan, K. B., C. M. G., of Colombo*, March 1928 :— "I thank you for the copy of your Tamil India. I have read it. It contains many things of interest to the general reader...."

7. *Mr. A. Muthiah Pillai, B.A., B.L.*, Vakil, and Secretary, Saiva Sabah, Palamcottah, Jan. 24, 1928 :—" I sincerely think that your *Tamil India* will be a valuable addition to the Sabah Library, and request you to send a copy for the said Library."

8. *Mr. Vishvanath V. Somasundram*, Hon. Secretary, the Colombo Hindu Dharma Samaj, Feb. 22, 1928 :—" I shall esteem it a great favour if you will oblige us by sending a copy of your valuable book 'Tamil India' at half-rate to our Free Reading Room by V. P. P. at your earliest convenience."

9. *Mudaliyar C. Arumugam*, Supreme Court, Colombo, Feb. 9, 1928 : " Kindly send me 2 copies of Tamil India, of which excellent book you are the distinguished author."

10. *Mr. N. V. Viswalingam*, Kuala Lumpur, Dec. 8, 1927 :—" Thanks for the two copies of your book 'Tamil India' which have duly reached me. I enclose herewith a Postal order for seven shillings and six pence in payment for same."

11. *Mr. N. Ramakrishna Mudaliar, Zamindar of Mahabalipuram*, Chingleput District, Oct. 21, 1927:—"Your work is of very rare merit. For the present I shall be glad to have *three* copies of it. You can send them by V. P. P."

12. *Mr. V. R. M. Chettiar, N. Pudur, Karaikudi*, Oct. 14, 1927: "Your 'Tamil India' is a valuable contribution to our National Series. It at once reveals the author's erudition in both languages—Tamil and English. It is an excellent guide for the European friends to know India aright. It looks like a challenge to Miss Mayo's *Mother India*."

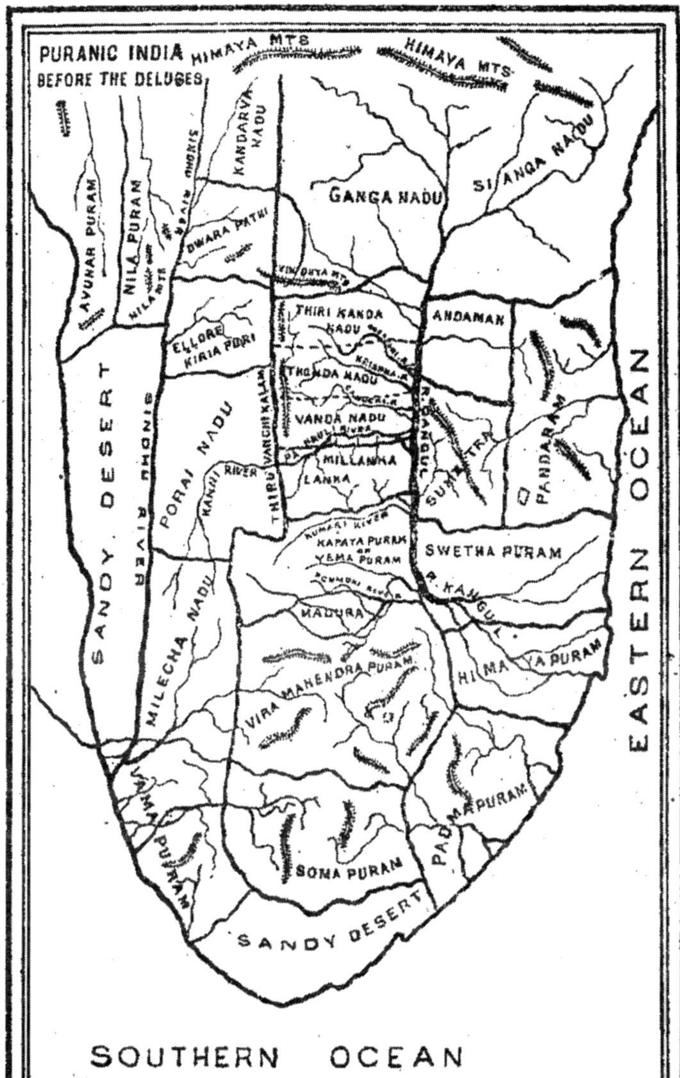
PURANIC INDIA
BEFORE THE DELUGES
HIMAYA MTS
HIMAYA MTS
KANDARVA NADU
GANGA NADU
SIANGA NADU
AVUNAR PURAM
NILA PURAM
DWARA PATHI
ANDAMAN
THIRI KANDA NADU
ELLORE KIRIA PORI
THONDA NADU
VANDA NADU
MILLANKA
LANKA
SANDY DESERT
SINDHU RIVER
PORAI NADU
KANHI RIVER
THIRU VANCHI KALAM
PANDARAM
KUMARI RIVER
KAPAYA PURAM or YEMA PURAM
SWETHA PURAM
R. KANGUL
MADURA
MILECHA NADU
HIMAYA PURAM
VIRA MAHENDRA PURAM
PADMA PURAM
SOMA PURAM
SANDY DESERT
SOUTHERN OCEAN
EASTERN OCEAN

RAVANA THE GREAT.

CHAPTER I.

LANKA.

Lanka, 'this utmost Indian isle', was in times of yore a portion of the main land of India. It was known as *Ilankai*, a province of Tamil-aham. (*Vide* Map I.) Situated between the Kumari and Pahruli rivers, it was a well-watered region and a prosperous country. When the second great deluge took place, a large portion of the Tamil country subsided, and Ilankai was separated by a broad channel of the sea. Since then it has remained as an island. It was at one time believed that it lay near the mouth of the Than Porunai or Tambraparni, and it was known to the Greeks and Romans as Taprobane.* " Seek the isle of Tamra-parni, gemmed upon the ocean wave". Taprobane was the name given by Megasthenes, the Greek Ambassador, sent by Seleukos Nicator of Syria to the Court of Chandragupta, the grandfather of Asoka.

**Vide* the Indian Patriot, Jan. and February 1913. 'The Original Inhabitants of India', and 'Nadars, their Origin'. The other names of the island are *Dhonacheri* for its wealth, *Dipuravanam*, (the island forest), *Cheran Divu* (because of its occupation by Cheras), and *Elam* or *Ela-mandalam*, which properly denoted the northern and eastern portions of it which had been occupied by the Tamils, long before the advent of king Vijaya (543 B.C.), with Ma-thottam as their metropolis.

In later times it was called Serendib, a corruption not of Sinhaladwipa, but of Cheran-divu, and Sirinduil. The name Ceylon has been variously accounted for: some say that it is a variant of Sinhalon or Singalam or wild cinnamon bark † while others affirm that it is Silan or Zeylan, which, in ancient Tamil, signified *tengu* or cocoanut palm.*

Whatever the origin or derivation of the name, there is no doubt that it is an isle of palms. It is mountainous or hilly with glens and glades in the south and sandy and shoaly in the north. It bears a close resemblance to the eastern shore of Travancore in its abundance of feathery cocoas, and of streams and streamlets, in the nature of its soil, which is more or less sulphurous, and in its climate and seasons. Lanka continues to be 'gay and green and glorious like the garden of the sky,' and 'golden and flower-bespangled like the gem-bespangled sea'. It was once called

†Vide Sen-Tamil, 1913. 'Lanka and the Tamil Sangams'.

*"The island of Tengu or cocoanut is Seeylon, which was so named from Silon in Malay and very ancient Tamil meaning cocoanuts." Nor is the island of Ceylon, against which the expedition of Rama was directed, called Taprobane or Tamraparni or *Palesimundu*, or *Palisimanta*, names anterior by some centuries to the Christian era. Nor is it even called by the name of *Sinhala*, (Seat of Lions) which name is connected with the occupation of the island by Vijaya, several centuries before our era. The name which Ceylon bears in the Ramayana is always the primitive, the most ancient Lanka."—(*Griffith*).

'Ratna' or 'Swarna' Bhumi for its pearls, gems and gold.

Lanka was also the name of the City of Ravana. It was securely built by the divine architect on the summit of Tirikuta: it was a hundred leagues long and twenty wide. It had stately domes and tall turrets, encircled by a wall built of blocks of gold, and by moats whose waters were bright with lily blossoms. The stately mansions rose like pale-hued clouds in the autumn skies; there were streets broad and bright, gates rich with the sheen of burnished gold and guarded by many a Raksha sentinel, and banners waved on every height. 'The courts were inlaid with turkises, and there were rows of crystal stairs and porticoes. The broad imperial street was bright and sweet with fresh blown flowers. The houses were decorated with varied ornaments, and about their crystal columns hung leaves and blossoms deftly strung together. The lords had their homes about the court, and the imperial palace, guarded by dames and the female retinue, armed with sword and spear and mace, had picture-halls and green bowers and lovely chambers and latticed windows bright with turkis and lazulite. Its polished floors were spread with fresh white and red buds and blossoms. In the spacious halls were lances, and bows, and shells, in fair array. Everywhere the softest carpets were spread, which were delightful to the sight and tread. The ladies bowers were supported by golden pillars, over which there were jewelled arches. The banquet-hall of the palace had rows of gold plates loaded with dainties of the earth, sea and air, and of cups wrought of gold, inwrought with gems. The royal dormitory had a crystal dais on which were golden couches and over which was a canopy famous for its artistry. Near the palace were lovely lakes full of lilies and lotuses. The palace looked so glorious that it matched in show an earthly paradise. The City of Lanka was, on the whole,

"A lovely city planned and decked
By heaven's creative architect,
Fairest of earthly cities meet
To be the Gods' celestial seat.

A glorious city fair to see
As Indra's Amravati;
A towering height of solid wall,
Flashing afar, surrounds it all;

Its golden courts enchant the sight,
And gates aglow with lazulite;
Steeds, elephants, and cars are there,
And drums' loud music fills the air.

Fair trees in lovely gardens grow,
Whose boughs with varied fruitage glow."

" In royal Lanka's glorious town ;
A city bright and rich, that showed
Well-ordered street, and noble road ,
Arranged with just division, fair
With multitudes in court and square"

" Vast is the city, gay and strong,
Where elephants unnumber'd throng,
And countless hosts of Raksha breed
Stand ready by the car and steed.
Four massive gates, securely barred,
All entrance to the city guard,
With murderous engines fixt to throw
Bolt, arrow, rock to check the foe.
And many a mace with iron head
That strikes at once a hundred dead.
Her golden ramparts wide and high
With massy strength the foe defy,
Where inner walls their rich inlay
Of coral, turkis, pearl display.
Her circling moats are broad and deep,
Where ravening monsters dart and leap.
By four great piers each moat is spann'd
Where lines of deadly engines stand.
In sleepless watch at every gate
Unnumbered hosts of giants wait,
And, masters of each weapon, rear
The threatening pike and sword and spear.

The City of Lanka is surmised to be the present Kandy, which is the very centre of Ceylon, beautiful with many fine temples and tombs and which was the metropolis of a dynasty of Kings for years.

Some say that the city was lost in the ocean, the city of "Lanka, girt by boundless ocean, is of royal towns the best, seated in her pride and glory on a mountain's towering crest"—(*Dutt*).

Ceylon, or the Isle of Palms, is a pear-shaped island, 271·5 miles long and 137·5 miles wide, about half the size of England. The Singalar are the aborigines of the island. The Sinhalese, occupying the south, are said to have immigrated from Bengal about 600 B.C., and the Tamils, found in the north, *i.e.*, Jaffna or Yal-panam, were immigrants 3000 years ago from the three east-coast districts of South India, *viz.* Tanjore, Madura and Ramnad. Now the capital of the island is Colombo, one of its large harbours, and the meeting place of many a nation of the world.

CHAPTER II.

RAKSHAS.

Who were the Rakshas? The Aryan poet has described the aborigines of Lanka as Rakshas, as monsters, demons and cannibals, 'with that contempt which has marked civilized conquerors in all ages.' "Rakshasas, according to the popular Indian belief, are malignant beings, demons of many shapes, terrible and cruel, who disturb the sacrifices and the religious rites of the Brahmans. It appears indubitable that the poet of the Ramayan applied the hated name of Rakshasas to an abhorred and hostile people and that this denomination is here rather an expression of hatred and horror than a real historical name"—(*Griffith*—Introduction to Ramayana.) The Aryans called themselves Gods, Suras, Yakshas, and their foes Asurar, Arakkar, Rakshasas, Nisa-sarar, Niruthar and so forth. Both were supermen, the former by the force of their penance and the latter by their strong constitution and physical prowess. The Aryan ascetics, not necessarily Brahmins, served as pioneers and spies against the Non-Aryans, whose forests they occupied without permission and of their own accord and whom to eradicate they attempted with the aid of kings who were powerful master-archers. The owners of Lanka and of the Dandaka forest including Janasthanam were the so-called Raksha King Ravana, his predecessors, his sister as Vicerene, and his cousins, who were Viceroy and General respectively.

Who were the Rakshas? They were of different clans, who had different status, and their main duty was protection. They were in fact wardens of the regions they lived in. They were owners of estates or kingdoms and kavalgars who protected the peace-loving people against the depredations of robbers, pillagers and plunderers. They were in colour and complexion black, as opposed to the Aryans who were bright or fair in colour and features. "It (the Ramayan) represents the Rakshas as black of hue, and compares them with black clouds and masses of black colly-rium; it attributes to them curly woolly hair and thick lips, it depicts them as loaded with chains, collars, and girdles of gold, and the other bright ornaments which their race has always loved, and in which the kindred races of the Soudan still delight. It describes them as worshippers of matter and force. They are hostle to the religion of the Aryans, whose rites and sacrifices they disturb and ruin." They were called night-rangers or rovers, because they patrolled at night. They were probably the ancestors of the Maravars, who are now either Zamindars and owners of large estates or protectors of people's lives and property, who claim and levy rates as *suthanthiram* or right and privilege. They formed the troops and body-guards of kings and fought valiantly for their kings and country. They were a hardy race of Titans. "Ravana and his tribe of Rakshas belonged to the *human* race and, in all probability, to the Marava community of the present day, thus forming a section of the Dravidians; and Ravana was the highest and the noblest specimen of humanity of his time. . . Even according to the mythological accounts of the Aryans, when Brahma (God) created water and men to guard it, the latter said *rakshanam*, 'we will protect.' Raksha was a man and he was created to be the guardian of property. In Southern India there is a class of stalwart dark-complexioned people called Maravars, meaning heroes, breathing martial spirit and always in search of adventures, and of whom every Dravidian has reasons to feel proud (notwithstanding the bad habits into which some of them have fallen of late). . . They not only formed the fighting strength of the early sovereigns, but were also engaged in policing the country in peaceful times, besides being rulers of provinces. From a certain noble duty they had to perform, and that during nights, the Aryans chose to nickname them and add a reproach to it."—(T.P.P.). Kamban has lines like the following in various places :

> " சேனைக்காவல போரை வருளர், பண்டு தேவர்
> வானைக்காவலு மானமு மாற்றிய மறவர்."—
> (யுத்தகாண்டம், இலங்கைகேள்விப்படலம், 62.)

> " திசைதொறு நிறுவின ருலகு சேரினும்
> பிசைதொழின் மறவரைப் பிறிதென் பேசுவ."—
> (ஊடி மந்திரப்படலம், 10).

" Such was the horror with which these aborigines inspired the Aryan Hindus that their always exuberant fancy transformed them into a race of cannibal giants, fiends, and wizards, possessed of supernatural powers and every evil, all that magic can lend, even to that of flying through space and assuming any form at will—thus transferring to them the attributes of the old Vedic cloud-demons whose place they took in the classical mythology of the race. These Rakshasas, whose horrible aspect and murderous wickedne make them the counter-part—or possibly th prototype—of our nurseries' Ogre, are des cribed as taking special delight in defilin sacrifices, disturbing the devotions of piou forest hermits, or leading them into unseeml temptations, carrying off pure and hol maidens, and opposing by force or wile the advance of the fire-worshipping, Soma-pres-sing friends of the Devas."—(*Vedic India*, p. 296). In the Ramayana they stand out as the main obstacle to Rama in his compaigns against Ceylon, as they formed "a compact population, brave, stubborn, and strongly organized." "Such the Dravidians are now, when they number over twenty-eight millions south of the Vindhya, and there is not the slightest reason to doubt that such in the main they were at the early time of their long patriotic struggle."

According to the Puranas, Brahma created the waters and formed certain beings to guard them. Some of these received the name of *Rakshas*. This was Agastya's reply to Rama, when the latter asked the former about the Rakshas' origin.

The Rakshas had been expelled from Lanka once by Vishnu in fulfilment of his word to the Devas, their foes. Ravana recovered it and the Rakshas occupied it once again. The Rakshas were a civilised race. They had cities and forts, palaces and parks, dancing halls and theatres, stables and chariot-houses. They sang solemn morning hymns of prayer and praise, and their priests were skilled in rite aad ritual and knew the Vedas and their six Angas—1 Siksha, the science of articulation and pronunciation, 2 Chandas, metre, 3 Vyakarana, grammar, 4 Nirukta, explanation of difficult words in the Vedas, 5 Jyotisha, astronomy or the Vedic calendar, and 6 Kalpa ceremonial (*Vide* Book V, C. 18 of Valmiki's *Ramayana*).

"Towards the southern extremity and in the island of Lanka (Ceylon) there existed undoubtedly a black and ferocious race, averse to the Aryans and hostile to their mode of worship, their ramifications extended through the islands of the Archipelago, and some traces of them remain in Java to this day"—(Signor Gorresio's Preface to his last and tenth volume of the Ramayana, translated into English by *Griffith*).

CHAPTER III.

LINEAGE.

Among the thirteen children of Brahma, Maricha, Manu, and Pulastia were three distinguished sons. Maricha's son was Kasipar. His sons were Indra, Varuna, and Surya. Surya's son was Yama. Manu had a son Prajapati, and Prajapati begot three sons—Agni, Vayu, and Soma or Chandra. Pulastia's son was Visravasu, and his son was Kuvera. These eight sons, who were closely related to each other, were the wardens of the eight points of the world's compass. Kuvera was in charge of the North, Yama of the South, Varuna of the West, Indra of the East, Vayu of the North-West, Agni of the South-East, Chandra of the North-East, and Surya of the South-West.

Kuvera or Visravana married four wives, who were Pushpóthkadai, Kalai, Kekasi and Devanini. The first wife bore five children—Karan, Mahodaran, Marichan, Prapa-thatthen, and Kumbi-nasi. Kalai begot Tirisira, Dushanan, Vidyut and Sivukan. Kekasi was the mother of Ravana, Kumbakarna, Surpanaka and Vibishana.

Brahma, the grandsire of the Universe, was the progenitor of the Yaksha and Raksha

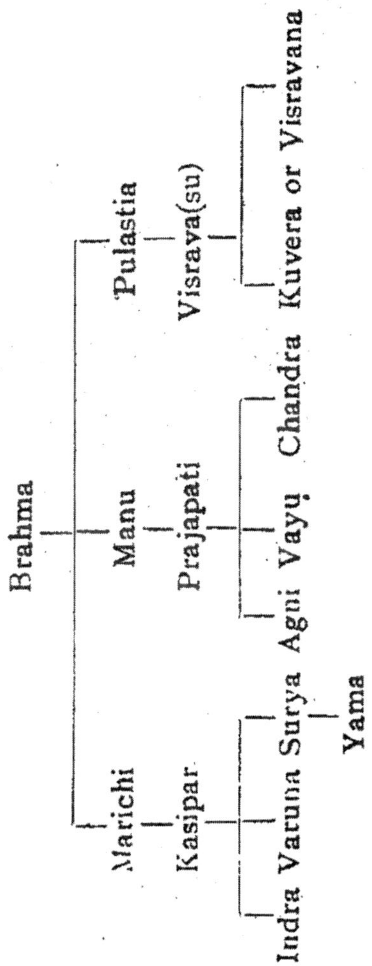
Brahma
Marichi
Manu
Pulastia
Kasipar
Prajapati
Visrava(su)
Indra
Varuna
Surya
Agni
Vayu
Chandra
Kuvera or Visravana
Yama

races, the founders of two great dynasties. Yaksha had two sons—Heti and Pra-heti. Heti had a son Vidyutkesan by Payáyai, sister of Kalan; Vidyutkesan married Sala Kadankadai and they begot Sukesan. Sukesan took to wife Devavati and begot three sons—Malyavan, Sumali, and Mali. Malyavan married Sundari and had many children by her, of whom Kalan, Durmukan, Virupakshan etc. were well-known. Sumali's children by Késthumathi *alias* Vanasa-Vilóchanai were a host of sons and daughters, of whom Prahatthan, Dandakan, Dumrakshan, *Kaikesi*, *Pushpothkadai* and *Kumbi-nasi* were well-known. Máli married Vasuthai, and their children were Nilan, Analan, Haran, Sambapathi, and others.

Yaksha

Heti — Pra-heti.

Vidyutkesan

Sukesan *m* Devavati

Malyavan — Sumali — Mali

Daughter-Kaikasi,
wife of Visrava and mother of Ravana.

Pulastia
- Deva Varuni
  - Visrava(su)
    - Visravana or Kuvera by *Devanini*
    - Karan, Mahodaran, Marichan, Prahathaithan, Kumbinasi by *Pushpothkadai*
    - Tirisira, Dushanan, Vidyut, Sivukan by *Kalai*
    - Ravana, Kumbakarna, Surpanaka, Vibishana by *Kekasi*

The three Rakshas, Malayavan, Sumāli and Māli, oppressed the Aryan ascetics (Gods), who resorted to Mahadeva for aid. Mahadeva's protege was Sukesa, the father of the three Raksha brothers, and he, therefore, advised the ascetics to pray to Vishnu. Vishnu promised to slay their enemies. A battle ensue between the champion of the god-like ascetic and the Rakshas. The latter were defeated and Māli was slain. Mālyavān renewed th contest in vain. The vanquished lived in Pathala or the nether regions and awaitec an opportunity for regaining their state anc power. It came in the days of Ravana, grandson of Sumāli by his daughter Kékasi.

It will now be clear that Ravana was a grandson of Pulastia on the paternal side and a grandson of Sumāli on the maternal side and that there was a commingling of the Yaksha and Raksha blood in his veins. In Book V Canto xxiii the Demons describe to Sita Ravana's noble descent:

> "One so strong and *great*, Pulastya's son,
> Pulastya—thus have sages told—
> Is mid the Lords of Life enrolled.
> Lord Brahma's mind-born son was he,
> Fourth of that glorious company.
> Visravas from Pulastya sprang,
> Through all the worlds his glory rang.
> And of Visravas' large-eyed dame
> Our King the mighty Ravan came."

CHAPTER IV.

LEARNING AND PIETY.

We have already referred to the Rakshas as well versed in the Vedas and their Angas and in Vedic ritual, and also to their matins or morning prayers. There are numerous passages in the Tamil classics pointing to Ravana, who was not only skilled in arms as became the lord of Lanka but richly endowed with holy love. 'Maraikal óre āyiram yan vallâne' *i.e.* 'I am a past master in a thousand marais.' So said he to Mayan, his would-be father-in-law, when the latter, pleased with his form and beauty, asked him who he was, and to what family he belonged, with a view to choose him as his daughter's husband. He knew by heart Rik and Samam and sang them, when occasions needed, in a touching, pathetic or melting manner. St. Appar has in his Tirumarais verses alluding to this fact. Vide I, 34 'Irukkisaikal pāda', I, 43. 'Kannalin' githam pāda', I, 49. 'Veda Githangal pāda', I 70 'patthu voi gitam pāda'. I 78 'thuttanai thuttu-thirthuchuvai-pada-Githam kétta', II. 31 'Githakinnaram pāda'. Similarly has St. Jnana Sambandhar referred to him as 'versed in

Vedas and in learning'. In his Tirumurais these verses exemplify it. II-92. 'Sama vedamore Githa móthía Dasamukan'. Ravana was a worshipper of Siva who taught him the Five Letters. III-119, 'Anjelutth-uraikka Arulinan'. Though a Titan of Titans, he never relied on himself as the Lord of Hosts, but on the efficacy of the boons offered to him. His piety is patent in St. 110 of Ravanan-vathai-padalam. It is said that, before he aimed his dart or used his missile, he worshipped Isa in his usual manner and performed puja. "Púsanai-tholil—purinthu-thān-Muraimayir-potrum-Isanai-tholuthu." By his austerities and penances for years he obtained boons from Siva, as longevity, and a broad bright sword, which gave him victory. II-54 'mukkódi vanal', 141 'valodu nal avarkku arul seitha'. An instance of the severity of his penance may be cited here. When Ravana promised his mother to equal his brother Kuvera in splendour, he went to the hermitage of Gokarna or 'the Cow-Ear' in the Kerala country in company with his brothers and performed austerity. After a long penance he plucked his heads one after another, so goes the legend, and threw them into the fire. When he was about to do it the tenth time, Brahma appeared and offered him three great boons, *viz.*, indestructibility by all creatures above or more powerful than man, recovery of his lost heads, and power to assume any shape he pleased, like Milton's spirits or fallen angels. He was so learned that he seldom acted without consulting wisdom. II, 3. 'Vitthakap-padai-valla arakkan.' He knew the arts of peace and war. He was proficient in music, vocal and instrumental. The six-stringed *yal* was his forte. With it made of his own nerves he pleased God Siva and won His Mercy and Grace. " Thām-aratthāl porā-thakai kol val padai, Kamarathal Sivan Karatthu Vānginan, " St. 160 of the same Ravana-vathai-padalam. It means that the grant of the sword (weapon), which was so sharp and keen that it could not bear filing, was made by Siva with his own hands on hearing his sweet strains or Kāmara. He was so expert a musician that he had a *yal* or Veenai inscribed on his flag, and hence poets have described him as 'Veenâi Kodiyóne,' or the possessor of the flag with the figure of the yal inscribed on it. " Eluthu-veenai-kol-ènthu-pathākai-mél, *i.e.*, over the lofty banner which bore the painted symbol of the lute (Stanza 21) and " Kodiyin-mélurai veenai " *i.e.* the lute inscribed on the high flag or standard (St. 34) *Ibid.* The onl person who is alleged to have excelled him i music (and magic) was the Sage Agastya A musical treatise by Rāvana, entitlec 'Rāvaneeyam', or the great Charmer i celebrated even to-day, and another, callec 'Ravana-bet,' or 'Ravana-patthiam' was compiled in later times, probably in commemoration of his unique attainments in tha soul-subduing as well as soul-stirring art

CHAPTER V.

MARRIAGE AND PROGENY.

In the Chapter on Lineage or Pedigree, it has been shown that Ravana, Kumbakarna, Surpanaka, and Vibishana were the four children of Visrava(su) by Kekasi, daughter of Sumali, a Raksha King. The eldest was Ravana, (so-named from the cry-rāva-uttered by him in his Kailasa exploit) * the mighty monarch of Lanka, and a great conqueror of worlds. He was tall as a mountain peak, his eyes were copper-coloured, and his teeth were bright like the moon. " His body bore the impress of wounds inflicted by all the divine arms in his warfare with the gods (Supermen). It was scarred by the thunderbolt of Indra, by the tusks of Indra's elephant, Airāvatha, and by the discus of Vishnu." As the lord of the utmost Indian isle, or Ilankai before its separation, he was known as *Thennavan.*

One day when Ravana went a-hunting, he came across a maiden, buxom, fair and debonair. She was the princess Mandothari,

* St. Appar III-79 : 'பத்திலங்குவாயாலும் பாடல் கேட்டுப் பரிந்தவனுக் கிராவணனென்றீந்த நாமத்தவனை.' St. 10, l. 3.

daughter of Mayan, who was the ruler of Yemapuri and an architect of wonderful skill, (*Vide* Map I) and sister of Māyāvi and Dhunthupi.

> "The chief artificer in place
> Was he of all the Dạnav race.
> He for a thousand years endured
> The sternest penance, and secured
> From Brahma of all boons the best,
> The knowledge Usanas* possessed.
> Lord, by that boon, of all his will
> He fashioned all with perfect skill."
>
> —*Bk. IV, C. 51.*

The beauty of her youthful face beamed a soft glory through the place, and young Ravana fell in love with her. She became his favourite queen, 'Ravan's first and eldest bride, slender-waisted, Queen of Lanka's state and pride.' She was a pious woman who merited Siva's favour. St. Manikkavachakar mentions and alludes to Siva's grace to Maṇdothari in *Quiyil Patthu*, St. 2 and *Thiru-Vārtthai*, St. 5 in this strain :

> "ஆர்கலிசூழ் தென்னிலங்கை யழகமர் வண்டோ
> தரிக்குப்
> போருளின்பமளித்த பெருந்துறை மேயபிரான்."

---

* A sage mentioned in the Vedas, identified with Sukra, the preceptor of the Asuras or Daityas.

"ஓங்குமதில் இலங்கையதனில் பந்தணைமேல்
விரலாட்கருளும் பரிசறவாரெம்பிரானவாரே."

They lived happily as Indra and Sachi, and their son was Meghanadha or the Roaring Cloud, who was afterwards called Indrajit for his victory over the sovereign of the skies.

In Kamban's Ramayana, or rather in Otta-Koothan's *Uttara-Kanda*, the father of this bewitching queen who was pleased with the handsomeness and juvenescence of Ravana asked the young man who he was, and what his ancestry, before he could make them man and wife. Lest he should be thought rude and uncivilised, he said that it was very hard to find suitable matches for the reason that the kith and kin of the spouses held different views on the choice of husbands. The members of the family of the bride desire that the bridegroom should be equal in birth and status to the bride; the father of the bride cares for intellectual breadth and moral height in the young man; her mother hankers after riches and broad acres; and the bride herself wishes that her sweetheart should be young and handsome. The possession in full of all the qualifications—handsomeness, youthhood, high culture, virtue and vast wealth—by any single individual is very rare, and the conclusion is that, as in the absence of any one of them, fault will be found with the choice, to bear a fair young maiden is very miserable. *Vide* Stanzas 60 and 61 of Ravanan's *Pirappu Padalam.*

"குலம்வேண்டு மென்றிருப்பார் குலத்துள்ளார்,
கல்வியினூற் குறையா ஞானப்
பலம்வேண்டு மென்றிருப்பார் தந்தைமார்,
பாரந்த பெருஞ் செல்வமுள்ள
தலம்வேண்டு மென்றிருப்பார் தாய்மார்கள்,
யவ்வனமு மழகுஞ் சார்ந்த
நலம்வேண்டு மென்றிருப்பார் காறுகுழற்
கன்னிமார் நலத்தின் மிக்கார்."—(60)

"பண்புடைய குடிப்பிறப்பும் பழிப்பில்லாப்
பேரழகும் பாரந்த கேள்வி
நுண்பொருளை நீரொழியப் பால்நுகரும்
அன்னம்போல் நோக்கித் தீரும்
எண்பொருளும் இந்நான்கு முடையாரைக்
கிடையாதிவ் வுலகந் தன்னில்
பெண்பெறுகை போலிந்தப் பெரியதுயர்
தானுண்டோ பேசுங் காலே."—(61)

Ravana, Dasanana, Dasagriva, Dasa-kanda, or Dasamuha, had, it is said, ten heads and twenty arms, but one body supported by only two legs. Divested of hyperbole, it meant that he was mighty in intellect and powerful in physique. Besides Indrajit, *alias* Ravani, the great Titan had other sons, who were great warriors. Athikayan and Akshan were two of them. Athikayan, tall of stature, wielded his arms powerfully, and Akshan, the youthful, brandished his bow, till they fell in battle. The names of three more sons are mentioned in the epic: Narāntakan, Devāntakan, and Tirisiras (probably the ruler of the regions about Trichinopoly or Thiri-sira-palli). His brother was the huge *Kumbakarnan*, who vied in might with Indra, the ruler of the skies. Neither Indra nor Varuna equalled him in his strength. He was the strongest of the Raksha warriors and stoutest-hearted midst the brave; he was stalwart, stout and tall like a mountain's beetling turret. The legend about him runs as follows: When Brahma was about to offer him a boon in appreciation of his penance, the gods interposed and begged that, under the guise of a boon, stupefaction might be inflicted on him. Brahma thought of Saraswati, who appeared, and, who, by his command, entered into Kumbakarna's mouth that she might speak for him. Under her influence the Titan desired sleep for months together and became a veritable Rip Von Winkle. When he recovered his consciousness, he perceived the trick but could not help it.

He ate much and quaffed plenty and sank in slumbers for six months at a stretch, with an interval of a single waking day every year.

> "He slumbering, free from care and pain,
> By Brahma's curse, for months has lain."
> "Strong Kumbakarna slumbering deep
> In chains of never-ending sleep."

He had to be roused from his drowsiness with war-drums thundering on all sides. His wife was Vachra swalai, who begot Kumbani, and Kumban.

The youngest of the male trio was Vibishanan, the reputed wise man. The Satvic quality is said to have reigned supreme in him. It is said that Truth and Virtue took precedence in his heart, and he counselled his brother and monarch against unrighteousness. Indrajit called him 'Traitor to thy king and kinsman, false to us in direst need.' He took to wife, Sarabai, daughter of Kai Dushanan, the Gandharva chieftain. Brahma offered him immortality in addition to virtue. Vibishana is praised as possessing 'the duteous mind, In needs unlike his giant kind.' There is reason to surmise from the paucity of the mention of any heirs of his to the throne of Lanka upon which the righteous Raksha was installed by Rama that he was childless. He is dubbed or canonised as an Alwār by the Rama-devotees or Vaishnavites. "The greatest of traitors, whom every Dravidian that has in him a spark of patriotism ought to execrate has been raised to the status and dignity of an *Alwar*"—(T. P. P.)

Their only sister was *Surpanaka*, with 'nails like winnowing fans.' 'Fierce Surpanaka—her of yore, The ten-necked tyrant's mother bore.' The Raksha-maiden, described as poor in beauty and plain in face, was given in marriage to Vitthuru-singan or Vithyucchavan or Kala-Kéyan. She called herself Kamavalli. Her son was Sampu-kumāran, born after his father's death. In a conflict with the brother Rakshas, Kala Keyar, Ravanan killed his brother-in-law unawares. In her widowed state Surpanaka was given for her maintenance the vast empire of Janasthanam and the Dandaka forest and was made Vicerene of it. She was helped by the statesmen and warriors, Kara and Dushana. She is depicted in the Epic as an ugly giantess. She fell in love with Rama in the forest and would have him as lord and husband, and said that Sita, pale and mis-shapen,

- Kekasi
  - Ravana *m.* Mandothari
    - 1 Indrajit or Ravani
    - The other sons
      - 2 Athikayan
      - 3 Akshan
      - 4 Tirisiras
      - 5 Narantakan
      - 6 Devantakan
  - Kumbakarna *m.* Vachra Swalai
    - 1 Kumbani
    - 2 Nikumban
  - Surpanaka *m.* Vitthuru-Singan
    - Sampukumaran
  - Vibishanan *m.* Sarabai
    - *Nil*

was scarcely a warrior's worthy wife and prayed to him to consecrate his gallant life to herself, a nobler, lordlier female, so that they together might range the woodlands and prove the joys of dalliance. In response to her passion, the chivalrous young warrior 'cleft her nose and either ear when she came alone, leaving on the way Kara and the doughty Dushana, by Rama's love emboldened.' Here follows a dark picture of her by the poet, Valmiki.

> "She, grim of eye and foul of face...
> She, of unlovely figure...
> She, whose, dim looks disordered hung...
> She, whose fierce accents counselled fear...
> She, whose dire form with age was dried...
> She, whose false lips maintained the wrong....
> She, cruel-hearted, stained with sin,...
> She, hideous fiend, a thing to hate."...
>
> (*Bk. III, C. 17*).

CHAPTER VI.

EXPLOITS.

The first great exploit of Ravana was the recovery of his ancestral possession of Lanka. Reference has already been made to Vishnu's exterminating invasion of the island and to the expulsion of the Raksha rulers to the underworld. How it was regained is related as follows. "Sumali with his family lived for a long time in Pathālā, while Kuvera dwelt in Lanka. He once happened to visit the earth, when he observed Kuvera going in his chariot to see his father Visravas. This led him to consider how he might recover his own fortunes. He consequently desired his daughter Kekasi to go and woo Visravas, who received her graciously. She became the mother of the dreadful Ravana, of the huge Kumbakarna, of Surpanaka, and of the righteous Vibishana, who was the last son. These children grew up in the forest. Kumbakarna went about molesting Rishis. At a subsequent time when Kuvera went to pay his respects to his father, Kekasi took occasion to urge her son Ravana to strive to become like his step-brother in splendour' Whereupon Ravana repaired to Gokarna and practised austerities at very great self-sacrifice. Having obtained boons, Ravana deputed Prahasta as envoy and he himself marched to Lanka with a large army. At the sight of his brother and his formidable forces, Kuvera consulted his father, who advised him to give up the city and the state to Ravana. It was done accordingly.

The next great adventure of Ravana was for the capture of *Pushpaka Vimana* or the Flowery Car, which was owned by Kuvera. It took place in the following circumstances. When the rishis who were looked upon as political spies occupied the aranya, which was part and parcel of the dominion of Ravana, and performed animal sacrifices in the name of God which were abhorrent to the Rakshas and professed wondrous powers, the Rakshas, in duty bound to guard it, oppressed them. Kuvera, at one with them, despatched a message to Ravana, his step-brother, to stop such oppressions. As it savoured more of command than request and was prejudicial to his interest, he resented it and led a large force against Kuvera. In the battle that ensued, Manipatra, the field-marshal of Kuvera, was slain, and Kuvera was not only defeated or overthrown but deprived of his aerial car.

In the words of Ravana, Bk. III, C. 48.

"Vaisravan once, my brother, wrought
To ire, encountered me and fought,
But, yielding to superior might,
Fled from his home in sore affright....
I made the vanquished king resign
The glorious car which now is mine—
Pushpak, the far-renowned, that flies
Will-guarded through the buxom skies,
Celestial hosts by Indra led
Flee from my face disquieted."

It may be noted that in times ancient there were sky-cars which were not driven by steam or electricity as the zeppelins or aeroplanes of to-day, but by will-power, which the rishis and rakshas seem to have possessed in plenty.

Another exploit of note was his invasion of the kingdom of departed spirits and his terrific battle with King Yama, the Just, whom he defeated. It was followed by his reduction of Bhogavati ruled by Vāsuki and by the subjugation of the Nagas. Ravana then attacked the imperial seat of Varuna in his absence and triumphed over his sons who did battle with the invader.

His two invasions of Ayodhya, once to subdue Anaranian, and the next time to check the pride of Mām-Dhātha, its monarch, in which the former was vanquished and the latter entered into a treaty with Ravana, at the entreaty of Gālava and Pulastia, are noteworthy.

Passing by his victories over the Gāthi (Visvamitra's father), Maruttha in the hall of sacrifice, Mayan, Dhuth-chandan and others and looking over his discomfitures in the conflicts with Vāli, Kārtha-Veeryan and Nivātha-Kavasar and his peace-makings with them at the instance of great men, we come to his remarkable feat of trying to uproot Kailasa for having blocked the passage of his marvellous aerial car. The legendary account is that Uma trembled at the mountain being shaken to its foundations and embraced her lord for safety, who pressed his foot on the mountain's crest and thereby crushed the head and limbs of Ravana. Immediately the hero chanted Sāmam and tuned his yal, which delighted the Lord so much that He pardoned his affront and blessed him with long life and with the gift of an invincible and ever-triumphant sword.

His last great exploit which proved fatal to him and to his race was the abduction of Sita. The immediate cause of it was the barbarous mutilation of Surpanaka, Ravana's sister, by Lakshmana. The other causes were the unauthorised occupation of the Dandaka forest by rishis, their inhuman and unseemly sacrifices tending to prejudice the prevalent modes of faith and ritual in the land, and, above all, their endeavour to make the forest their own by seeking the aid of sovereigns who had no earth-hunger at all. Though the prime mover and *teterrina causa belli* was the sister of Ravana, the abduction was made in due accordance with the rules of the Tamilian modes of warfare. It is ridiculous on the part of the Aryan Chronicler to attempt to whitewash the acquiescence of Rama or the heinous action of Rama's brother-exile by saying that the Vicerene threatened to eat Sita, as if she were a cannibal. Who would believe the statement that, passion-ridden, she went to Rama unaccompanied or alone, without a previous clandestine love with the prince of Ayodhya? It is very likely that Sita was shrewd enough to discover or detect the secret love and that Rama professed innocence to satisfy his wife and stand in her good graces. Whatever the cause, the carrying away of any object near and dear to the enemy with a view to give him an occasion for showing his valour and redeeming it was the practice in vogue in the Tamil country. So Ravana's procedure was quite in consonance with it. The wily Aryan prince, dragged into the conflict by the praises and prayers of the ambitious rishis in the first instance, sought the aid of the exiles, the wife-lorn Sugriva, and his warrior-in-chief Hanuman, described in the epic as beings endowed in contempt with caudal appendages, to make a quest of the ravished Sita. Would a love-sick Titan place Sita in the Asoka grove under the guardianship of women who were his kith and kin, and beg of her to requite his love and marry him? It seems extremely improbable that such was the case. Did Rama directly pursue Ravana to recover Sita? He indulged in moanings and mournings unworthy of a master archer. But for the Dravidian Hanuman who played the incendiary and the medicine man and for the treacherous Vibishanan who ran away from his brother, informed Rama of the vulnerable points of his foe and of the city of Lanka, victory and wife-recovery would have been out of the question. The Aryan mode of conquest was and is 'Divide and Conquer'. Ravana fought as a warrior and fell, and so did his brother Kumbakarna, and his son Indrajit. All honour to them.

> " Ravan ne'er can yield or bend,
> And be it vice or virtue, I
> This nature never will belie"—(Bk. VI, C. 36.)

Among the exploits of Ravana have been included some of his love escapades. The Aryan Chronicler enumerates them and lays special stress upon them with a view to establish Nemesis or the Law of Retribution for sinful acts committed by him. The Mysteries of the Court of London and of Paris cite countless instances of vicious excesses in royal families. If hot blood in an ordinary individual overleaps cold decrees, the royal blood has a licence in the matter. If, in a country where polygamy prevails, liaisons are very frequent and common, they must ride rough-shod in places where monogamy is strictly enjoined and purity in woman is sternly enforced. The Rakshas had the privilege of taking many wives and of maintaining a harem. In these circumstances rapes and ravishments would be unnecessary and uncalled for. In all countries poor women often throw themselves in the way of Kings for favour of acceptance and many are caught, like moths, by the glare of royal pomp and circumstance. Vedavati, the young and beautiful but poor daughter of Rishi Kusadhwaja, had been dedicated by her father to Vishnu or Narayana. Ravana is alleged to have touched the hair of her head with the tip of his finger, when she entered the blazing fire. Rambha, wife of Nālakūpara, was forced by Ravana, and her husband cursed him that his head should split should he take any woman by force. Enamoured of Lakshmi, in Pāthālā, he went thither, but was driven away. Similarly, the wife of Śambān was approached by the lord of Lanka, who, captured by her husband, was released at the intercession of his queen Mandothari, who had the grace of Siva.

CHAPTER VII.

GOVERNMENT.

The island of Lanka was primarily Ravana's Kingdom. It is said that Agastya forbade Ravana by the marvellous power of his music and magic from acquiring any spot in the surviving Tamilaham. His son, Tirisira, owned territory on the banks of the Cauveri. Janasthanam and the Dandaka forest were under his absolute control. He was their overlord. His sister Surpanaka in her widowed state was their Vicerene, assisted by Kara, her prime minister, to carry out her behests, and Dushana to guard her and her vast empire with a force of 14,000 choicest warriors. The government of Lanka was in his own hands. He had an advisory body or council, composed of the ablest and most experienced statesmen and warriors, and consulted it in times of need. He had ministers, ambassadors, and spies who were true and loyal to him. Though he gave his ear to them, he always acted on his own decision and was every inch a King. He was ubiquitous, and his influence was felt everywhere, far and near.

"Where none is King, the sower's hand
Casts not the seed upon the land;
The son against the father strives;
And husbands fail to rule their wives;
In kingless realms no princes call
Their friends to meet in crowded hall;
No joyful citizens resort
To garden trim or sacred court......
In kingless lands no law is known,
And none may call his wealth his own.
Each preys on each from hour to hour
As fish the weaker fish devour......
As in the frame of man the eye
Keeps watch and ward, a careful spy,
The monarch in his wide domains
Protects the truth, the right maintains.
He is the right, the truth is he,
Their hopes in him the well-born see.
On him his people's lives depend,
Mother is he, and sire, and friend.
The world were veiled in blinding night,
And none could see or know aright,
Ruled there no King in any state
The good and ill to separate—(Bk. II, C. 67).

Primogeniture governed the succession
he throne.

"Eldest son of the eldest brother—such the maxim we own,—
Worthy of his father's kingdom, doth ascend his father's throne"—(*Dutt*).

This ancient custom was ruthlessly broken by the Aryans who followed the principles of expediency and compromise. The installation of Ravana's surviving brother in preference to his sons who were yet in the land of the living illustrates the statement. Sugriva was placed on the throne of Kishkinda rather than Angadha, the son of Vali. This is another notable instance of the violation by the Aryans of the law of succession which bound the Rakshas.

As Ravana governed his country well, there was internal peace, and no feud. His foreign policy was equally good and admirable. He was friends with his brother monarchs, and no foreign aggression is mentioned or alluded to in the epic. When Hanuman thought of the four expedients of conciliation, gifts, disunion, and force, which were commonly resorted to for vanquishing an enemy or for making him come to terms, he deemed it wise to adopt the fourth, as the trial of the other expedients would not, in his opinion, succeed with the loyal subjects of Ravana.

> " These dwellers in the giant's isle
> No arts of mine can reconcile.

I cannot bribe: I cannot sow
Dissension mid the Rakshas foe.
Arts, gifts, address, these fiends despise;
But force shall yet their King chastise"—
(Bk. V, C. 51).

Besides the island and Janasthanam, Ravana held suzerainty over ten or more isles, which contributed thousands of faithful and loyal fighters to him in times of war. *Vide* stanzas 9 to 23, *Padai-Katchipadalam,* C. 29, Yuddhakanda. The whole military strength of Lanka's lord was a thousand Vellam, vellam being a myriad or a very large number.

Ravana was the head of the civil, judicial, military and spiritual administration of his vast and extensive realm, and obedience, not through mere fear but out of love for the safety and peace-giving monarch, was the bond of his rule. Harmony prevailed, and no hitch.

The Raksha government of Lanka had a short interregnum of Yaksha rule when Kuvera bore sway during the minority of Ravana. How long and when Ravana reigned is not known; everything is pre-historical: Ravana was a contemporary of Rama. Subsequent to the fall of the Rakshas, the island seems to have been occupied and ruled by the much civilised and heroic Nagas, whose kings were known as Naga-royar and who had held dominion all over India up to the Himalayas. The towns, Nāgapattinam, Nāgapuram, Nāgarkoil etc. testify to that fact. The first prince of Thondai-mandalam was the offspring of a Naga princess and a Chola King. Yalpanam or Manal-Divu (Manatti--sandy or shoaly island) had borne the name of Naga-Divu or Dwipa. When the Naga rule came to an end, the vanquished Naga kings probably settled permanently in the said isle, and in the Nainar dwipa, and in a division of Vindhanai. In ancient Tamil classics occur the names of Naga rulers among the Sangam poetic fraternity, as Mudi Nagar or crowned Nagan, Ila-Nagar, or Young or Prince Nagan, and others.

After the conversion of the island to Buddhism, the government was more or less Buddhistic, and the Mahavamso enumerates seventy-seven kings, beginning with Vijaya, (the first ruler of the Sinhala dynasty from the Gangetic valley,) between B. C. 543 and A. D 445. Lanka was in historical times frequently invaded by the Kalinga, Chola, Chera and

Pandyan kings, including the Nayak rulers. At one time it was known as Cheran-divu on account of its occupation by a Chera king. The History of Lanka mentions Vikramaraja Singan as having waged an atrocious war with the English. He was the 165th ruler and probably the last. In 1815 the Kandyan ruler was deposed, and deported to Vellore, and the island became a crown colony.

CHAPTER VIII.

WAR IN LANKA.

War has been described by the poet as the last argument of noble kings'. The causes of the war in Ceylon have already been adverted to. The 'missionary, merchant, monarch' has been wittily said to form the different stages in the conquest of a country. The missionary goes to preach his religion, and, under the garb of his holy or sacred function, puts on record the state of the land in its political, economic and social aspects, whither he has made his way. The merchant follows him and carries on trade with it. The produce and wealth of the region are exploited and reported upon to the mother country. For the sake of establishing religion and draining the resources thereof, the flag of the nation to which he belongs is put up at last. War is declared on some pretext or other, and is followed by conquest and annexation. In ancient India the different stages were *rishi*, *ritual* and *rupture*. The rishis or anchorites built their asrams wherever they pleased and performed sacrifices and observed rituals or rites and ceremonies obnoxious to their peaceful neighbours and provoked them into rupture and called in the aid of powerful monarchs to withstand oppression. In short, they let loose the dogs of war. In his Calcutta University Carmichael lectures delivered in 1918, Mr. D. R. Bhandarkar writes of the work of the rishis in these terms: "The ancient Rishis were not mere inert thinkers, but were active, though not aggressive, propagators of their faith" (p. 17). "Rishis took a most prominent but unobtrusive part in the Aryan colonisation and the diffusion of Aryan culture" (p. 19.) "To the south of the Vindhya, there were many Brahmin anchorites who lived in hermitages at different places and performed their sacrifices before Rama penetrated Dandakāranya and commenced his career of conquest.....The Rishis were always to the forefront in the work of colonising Southern India and introducing Aryan civilisation. Among them Agastya was the only Rishi, who fought with the Rakshas and killed them. The other rishis, like true missionaries, never resorted to the practice of retaliation, though they believed rightly or wrongly that they had the power of ridding themselves of their enemy. One of them distinctly said to Rama: 'It is true that, by the power of our austerities, we could *at will* slay these goblins; but we are unwilling to nullify (the merit of) our austerities" pp. 20-21. (Ramayana, Bk. III C. 10 ll 13-4). The rishi Visvamitra implored Dasaratha to send his son Rama with him southward to ward off or extinguish the Raksha troubles. Later, when Rama was exiled, he spent months and years in the hermitages in the Dandaka forest. In his wanderings in this Aranya, he came across Surpanaka, the widowed princess and Vicerene. She appeared before Rama as a most lovely girl, her glossy hair ornamented with flowers, with gold bangles tinkling round her slender ankles and wrists. In the conversation that ensued, Rama addressed her thus: "Beautiful maid, I am grateful to you for your kindness; but, as you see, I am already married, and you would be angry if you had to be the lesser wife. But there is my brother Lakshmana, handsome and young. He is a suitable husband for you.' When Surpanaka approached him, he said "Lovely maid, you cannot want a slave like me as your husband. I am the slave of my brother. He is handsome, strong, and a great warrior. You must marry him, and he will love you so much that he will desert his present wife.' She thought that Lakshmana was serious and returned to Rama. His tantalisation and veiled mockery * provoked her, and he felt that it was ill-jesting with a woman in power. In her forlorn state it was natural for her to have cast glances or side-long looks of love at the Aryan exiles. Their eyes met and spoke eloquently. The elder Kshatrya prince was evidently bewitched by the lordlier Raksha dame, and polygamy among the Kshatryas was nothing strange. According to Tholkappiam, a Kshatrya was entitled to marry three wives, and monogamy did not hang upon his neck like a nether mill-stone. The plea of conjugal fidelity by Rama sounds hollow under the circumstances. He probably dreaded Sita's suspicion, discovery, or detection of the love-intrigue. To pass for a spotless husband in the eyes of his spouse, the banished hero and rishi-champion would have none of Surpanaka; he told her to go to Lakshmana, knowing full well that the chivalrous young man would deal harshly by her. She suffered mutilation at his hands, and bewailed her lot. Ravana's blood boiled when he saw her bereft of her nose and ears. The slaying of Kara and Dushana and 14,000 picked

* "[illegible]."

Rakshas by Rama had already infuriated him. Ravana could bear no more the insult added to the injury. He carried away Sita in accordance with the war practice in vogue in the Tamil land and expected that her life-partner would pursue and redeem her Instead of pursuing the ravisher himself, he sought the alliance of Sugriva who was wife-less and in like circumstances. He deputed parties of his men in quest of Sita. The Dravidian hero, Hanuman, with Sugriva, an exile, volunteered his service, bent upon smashing the heroic Vali by hook or by crook. He made a long tour in the South and crossed the sea and set the City of Lanka on fire at night. Was it a knightly deed? It was an act of the knights of the highways. After the fire-devastation of the city, on the advice of the brother-traitor Vibishana, Hanuman escaped from the island with his skin and teeth safe but did not bring Sita with him. After the city was in ruins, Rama had no great difficulty in rescuing her. She was in the Asoka grove, well-guarded and well-nursed. Rama thought he could take an easy walk over the intervening sea and have Sita back. War was proclaimed. Ravana held a council of war and sought advice.

For 'wisest monarchs act on counsel from his men for wisdom known, and wisest counsel comes from courtiers who in holy lore unite'. 'From counsel, sages say, the root springs victory, the most glorious fruit'. He pressed the Council for an early reply lest the Vanar host should invest the island. Prahasta, the Prime Minister, said that his gallant Raksha forces would stand by him in his need, that Hanuman stole like a craven spy, and that the lord of Lanka had nothing to fear in the gory field of battle with the Vanars. Next Durmukha spoke in fury, and wound up his speech with the statement that his single arm would attack and drive the daring Vanars back, without need of gathered forces. The third speaker was Vajra-danshtra. He suggested two schemes. One was that he would with his mace slay Sugriva and drive away the helpless hermit brothers, and the other that his gallant soldiers should disguise themselves as Bharat's men and fall upon the enemy with mace and bloody sabres until there was left no survivor. The brave Nikumbha, son of Kumbakarna, arose and cried in fury that he alone would take the field and see the foemen down, one and all. Vajra-hana, iron-jawed, advised the king in a similar strain. Vibishana warned his brother against the impending doom of his raksha race and prayed to him to restore the captive and thereby avert the catastrophe. 'Doubly armed is the hero—he who battles for the right'. 'Faithful friend but fiery foeman is Dasaratha's son'. 'Righteousness becomes the brave, cherish peace and cherish virtue, and thy sons and daughters save'. Moved to sudden wrath, by the praise of his enemy's valour, Ravana dismissed his cowardly and dastardly brother from the Council hall. Then came Kumbakarna, who condemned the rape in strong terms, but who would live or die with his brother and monarch, which was his duty. He would fight his monarch's battle and would face his brother's foe. He would be true to brother and to monarch, were he right or were he wrong. He said:

> "But, Ravan, as the deed is done,
> The toil of war I will not shun".

Indrajit assured his father of victory and added that he, victor over Trilokanatha, would not yield to a homeless human foe. After giving a patient ear to all the councillors, Ravana was disgusted with the lurking envy of Vibishana and with his vaulting ambition and decided to meet the foe in open combat and give him a chance to recover his wife by his feats of strength.

Vibishana fled to where Rama was, accompanied by four captains of the band—Analan, Anilan, Aran, and Sampāthi. Sugriva took him for a spy from the giant host and Angadhan entertained similar doubts. Sarabha also would try and test him. King Jāmbavān too suspected him and Mainda also cautioned Rama. The shrewd Hanuman said:

> "Vibishan comes no crafty spy:
> Urged by his brother's fault to fly,
> With righteous soul that loathes the sin,
> He fled from Lanka and his kin."

These words cleared up Rama's rising doubts, and he spoke thus :

> "The suppliant will I ne'er forsake,
> Nor my protecting aid refuse,
> When one in name of friendship sues,
> Though faults and folly blot his fame,
> Pity and help he still may claim".

Immediately Rama flattered Vibishana with the kingship of the island :

> "And thou shalt reign in Ravana's stead",

and Vibishanan was consecrated with sea-water amid shouts of 'Vibishanan, Lanka's lord', He burst out with words of zeal and enthusiasm ; for, in his exceeding joy, he could

not contain himself and betrayed the nature ‹
his inner man.

> " Thy conquering army will I guide
> To storm the city of the foe,
> And aid tbe tyrant's overthrow."

Spies were sent by Ravana to survey th
enemy's forces. Sardula reported ' A rushin
tide Ten leagues they spread from side t
side '. Suka, detected by Angadha as a sp
was taken captive and bound, but was release
at the intervention of Rama. So was Sara
Both told King Ravana :

> " Vibishan seized us, King, and fain
> His helpless captives would have slain,"

and praised Rama's generous heart and th
four undaunted and unparalleled chiefs of th
foe's forces—Sugriva, Vibishana, Rama, an
Lakshmana. Provoked by the reports, th
Lord of Lanka ordered his captains an
generals to be ready for valiant defence.

> " There in the centre, Rama cried,
> Be Angad's place by Nila's side.
> Let Rishabh of impetuous might
> Be lord and leader on the right,
> And Gandhamadhan, next in rank,
> Be captain of the farther flank,

Lakshman and I the hosts will lead,
And Jambavan of Ursine* breed,
With bold Sushen unused to fear,
And Végadarsi, guide the rear".

Thus marshalled, Rama's forces marched southward and surveyed the island from Suvela's peak. The sallies commenced in right earnest. The beleaugered city of Lanka was attacked by the serried ranks. Vanars and Rakshas fell in countless numbers. Indrajit, the first in his magic art, twice defeated both Rama and Lakshmana.

"Fastened by a noose of *Naga* forced by hidden foe to yield,
Rama and the powerless Lakshman fell and fainted on the field".

Dumraksha and Akampan were slain by Hanuman ; Vajra-danshtra was laid lifeless on the plain by Angadha ; and Prahasta was felled by the gallant Nila. Sugriva encountered Ravana and fainted beneath the furious shock of his foeman's arrows. The Vanara host fell in battalions. Hanuman came against Ravana whose mighty onset rolled Hanuman weltering in red blood upon the gory plain. Next fought the valiant Nila, and died. After Nila's fall Lakshmana challenged

* Of the bear.

Ravana to wage with him an equal stri e, when they closed in dubious battle. Wh n at last Ravana hurled his *Sakti*, the javelin of flaming splendour, which was given him by the gods in days of yore, the gallant Laksmana could not resist its consuming force and fell. At his fall Rama arose, but Ravana retreated. He sent Kumbakarna to the fra . At his sight the Vanars fled. Encouraged by Angadha, the Vanars sallied once agai . Kumbakarna struck down Hanuman and hurled down Rishabah, Nila, Saraba, Gavasha, and Gandha-madhan, chieftains of undying fame. Angadha met a similar fate, and Sugriva fared none the better. Lakshmana could not fight long with the huge warrio. Rama met him last and knocked off his hea with his piercing arrow. After his death, th sons of Ravana—Narantaka, Devantaka Tirisiras, Atikaya—came one after another met their death at the hands of Angadha Hanuman, and Lakshmana. Ravana wep for the slaughtered princes, but Indrajit, who had begun the Nikumbila, a wonderful sacrifice, sought the field against the exiled princes and used his magic art. Both felt desperate and made up their minds to die with dauntless hearts. In the third engagement Indrajit fell on the field of Nikumbhila, smitten by the unerring dart of Lakshmana. Ravana was taken by surprise and lamented woefully. 'The father wept the son.' Ravana sought a fitting revenge for his brave and noble son and called upon Mahodar and Virupaksha and Mahaparshwa to remember the death of Khara, Dushana, Kumbakarna, and Indrajit and do their duty. When the Raksha squadrons shook the earth beneath their tread, they had foul omens, and their hearts beat slow. Sugriva slew Mahodar and Virupaksha, and Angadhan felled Mahaparshwa. Ravana swept the ranks of war with more than mortal valour ; and, when he found his false brother battling by the foeman's side, he threw his mighty javelin at him. But Lakshmana saved him by his might. Ravana smote Lakshmana down by his *Sakti.* Hanuman played the Galen and brought healing herbs, whose juice brought the fallen warrior back to life. Ravana for the third time went to war. The dubious battle lasted long. Ravana used pike and club and mace and trident against the spear, sword and arrows of Rama, but he could not withstand Brahma's deathful weapon, wielded by Rama, which pierced his iron heart and laid him low and lifeless.

Thus fell the mighty Lord of Lanka, by th hand of a *human* foe, the Raksha host send ing forth a wild terrific yell, while othe voices breathed 'champion of gods, wel done, well done'. He who had borne a charmed life died with harness on his back and his death was glorious indeed !

CHAPTER IX.

DEATH AND FUNERAL.

What was his age when Ravana fell? He was verily above fifty years old. But the epic is silent on the point. When Vibishana saw his brother slain, his ambition—veiled heart could not contain its woe. Is not blood thicker than water? The brotherly instinct spoke. The death of the man, first in war, first in peace, and first in the hearts of his countrymen, was bewailed, and the falsely true brother, who believed that the tree of liberty grew only when watered by the blood of tyrants, broke out in lament, though it seemed judas-like, a mock lamentation.

"O hero, bold and brave! he cried,
Skilled in all arms, in battle tried,
Spoiled of thy crown, with limbs outspread...
Woe for the giant's royal tree,
Whose stately height was fair to see.
His buds were deeds of kingly grace,
His bloom the sons who decked his race.
With rifled bloom and mangled bough
The royal tree lies prostrate now."—

(B.K. VI Ch. III.)

Did the usurper live long to enjoy the fruits of his treason or perfidy? Did he transmit, or had he any posterity to whom to transmit, the diadem and sceptre wrongly bestowed? There are reasons for us to believe that he had neither blessing. He must have felt in his dying days,

> " Upon my head they placed a fruitless crown,
> And put a barren sceptre in my gripe, *hand*,
> Thence to be wrenched *with an unlineal*
> *No son of mine succeeding.*"

Mandothari, Ravana'a spouse, wept bitter tears over the corpse of her lord and husband, the greatest soldier of the world, her 'plated Mars,' 'the arm and burgonet of men.'

> " Hast thou fallen, king and consort, more than Gods in warlike might,
> Slain by man, whom bright Immortals feared to face in dubious fight?
> Woe to me! the sad remembrance haunts my tortured bosom still,
> Of our days on famed Kailasa or on Meru's golden hill,
> Gone the days of joy and gladness, Mandothair's days are done,
> Since her lord and king and husband from her dear embrace is gone!"

A CHASTE WIFE DOES NOT SURVIVE HER HUSBAND FOR A MINUTE.

"போர்மகளைக் கலைமகளைப் புகழ்மகளைத்
தழுவியகை பொறாமை கூரச்
சீர்மகளைத் திருமகளைத் தேவர்க்குந்
தெரிவரிய தெய்வக் கற்பின்
பேர்மகளைத் தழுவுவா னுயிர்கொடுத்துப்
பழிகொண்ட பித்தா பின்னைப்
பார்மகளைத் தழுவினையே திசையானைப்
பணையிறுத்த பணைத்த மார்பால்"

"The hand that embraced the goddess of War, the goddess of Learning, the goddess of Fame, at the instigation of jealousy, longed to embrace the daughter of virtue and fortune, the divinely chaste lady unseen even by the gods, and this led to the loss of life and the commission of sin. O madman, thou, who hadst by thy bravery conquered the elephantine guardians of the *airts*, liest in the embrace of mother Earth."

Her life goes out the moment she hears that her lord is no more; for, with him all her bliss comes to an end.

"கணவனையிழந்தாள் கடையகத்தாளே
கணவனையிழந்தாள் கடையகத்தாளே"

that is, she who has lost her husband is the last of the household. So cried Kannaki, the heroine of Silappathikaram to the King of Madura when he condemned her husband to instant death on a false charge of theft at the instance of a roguish goldsmith.

One hero appreciates another. Rama said:

> "The warrior king has nobly died,
> Intrepid hero, firm through all,
> So fell he as the brave should fall."
> "Yet for the fallen warrior plead
> The dauntless heart, the valorous deed,.
> Let him who ne'er had brooked defeat,
> The chief whom Indra feared to meet,
> The ever-conquering lord obtain
> The honours that grace the slain."—(C. 113.)

and bade the funeral rites and obsequial honours duly paid by Vibishanan and the rest. They heaped sandalwood, laid fragrant garlands and precious scents, arrayed the fallen leader in the richest robes, decked him with pearl and coral ornaments, laid the corpse upon a golden litter surrounded by weeping queens and sorrowing Rakshas, hung flowers and pennons thereon and sang the monarch's praise. The golden litter or bier was lifted and borne to the burning ghat or cremation ground with blazing holy or sacred fire. Vibishanan led the slow procession of the dead followed by the sad widowed multitude. On the piled sandal logs and scented wood, the corpse was set, offerings were made to propitiate the shade, Brahmans chanted mantras, an altar was formed southward on the eastern side, oil and curds were shed on the dead man's shoulder, rich vesture was laid on the corpse, parched grain was strewn over it, a goat of inky darkness was slain as a sacrifice, and the funeral pyre was lighted by Vibishana. When the zephyrs gently blowing fanned the bright and blazing fire, the mourners left the burning ground after due ablutions. The sacrifice of a goat at the funeral was probably an Aryan custom.

CHAPTER X.

CHARACTER.

The character of Ravana has been much vilified as a love-sick Titan. Ravana carried off Sita as a war-prize and treated her with courtesy, decorum and respect. Had he been passion-ridden, as alleged by the chronicler and purana-writer, he could have committed outrage or done her to death in case of obduracy. He did neither, when Surpanaka suggested,

> ' Let Sita of the faultless frame
> Be borne away and be thy dame.'

Ravana acted upon it for the reasons mentioned herebelow.

> " He (Rama) sought the wood with fair pretence.
> Of truthful life and innocence,
> But his false hand my sister left
> Mangled, of nose and ears bereft.
> This Rama's wife who bears the name
> Of Sita, in her face and frame
> Fair as a daughter of the skies—
> Her will I seize and bring the *prize*
> *Triumphant* from the forest shade."[1]

Accordingly he skylarked Sita, Rama's 'darling wife, dearer to Rama than his life.'

> "Then Ravan raised her up, and bare
> His captive through the fields of air."

Sita was a dark beauty, of the furrow sprung, a Dravidian woman who cared for her chastity more than her life. Ravana bore sway over almost all India, Mount Kailas not excepted, and was called Thennavan, a man of the south, for Ilankai had been a province of Tamilaham in pre-diluvian times. He was a Dravidian, a Tamilian in particular. His mother tongue is nowhere indicated, though he is represented as a Sanskrit scholar. Hanuman spoke to Sita in a Dravidian language which was intelligible to her and not in Sanskrit. In his *Lectures on the Ancient History of India*, on the period from 650 to 325 B.C. delivered in 1918 by Mr. D. R. Bhandarkar, M.A., F.A.S.B., Carmichael Professor of Ancient Indian History and Culture, Calcutta University, he has, pp. 25—8. "It is, indeed, strange how the Aryan failed to supplant the Dravidian speech in this (southern) part of India, though it most successfully did in Northern India, *where I have no doubt the Dravidian tongue prevailed before the advent of the Aryans.* This will be seen from the fact that 'Brahui, the language of the mountaineers in the Khanship of Kelat in Beluchistan, contains not only some Dravidian words, but a considerable infusion of distinctively Dravidian forms and idioms.'*......It is also a well-known fact, accepted by all scholars, that there are many Sanskrit words, which are all Dravidian........And this will confirm the conclusion that the Dravidian tongue was prevalent in North India before the Aryans came and occupied it. The same conclusion is forced upon us by an examination of the vernaculars of North India........*No reasonable doubt can therefore be entertained as to the Dravidian speech once being spoken in North India.*" We may add that Tamil, being the mother of the Dravidian languages, prevailed throughout India in pre-historic times. This digression is necessary to show that Sita was a Dravidian lady, a worshipper of Siva,—a fact confirmed by her worshipping in a Siva shrine in the place now called Ramesvram immediately after she landed on the eastern shores of India. The place, which was rightly Ravanesvaram, came to bear the name, Ramesvram, because Rama worshipped Iswara there,

* Caldwell, *Grammar of the Dravidian Languages.* Introduction, pp. 43—4.

though it is said that he cooped a *linga* of sand for the purpose. Why he worshipped a linga may not be intelligible to lay minds; his worship of the linga might seem ridiculous to an unhistorical reader who views the question from the point of Rama being an incarnation or a devotee of Tirumal. To continue the characterisation of Ravana. When Sita was in his clutches, he merely made overtures to her. Sita disdained them. As a Dravidian, Ravana would not touch her, unless she yielded.

> " But I with rude hands will not touch
> A lady whom I love so much ",

This, his chivalrous and magnanimous behaviour, is in striking contrast with the conduct of the Aryan prince who cleft Surpanaka's nose and ears, despite the Aryan chronicler's picture of the Dravidian princess as a she-cannibal. Ravana, had he been a rude monster, would have done Sita to death when his sons and kinsmen were slain by Rama and his allies and the island was desolated. But Ravana forbore doing any such wicked act of revenge. So chivalrous was he that he once set out for vindicating the honour of Kumbinasi, but he gave it up at her entreaty.

We have shown in the preceding pag that Ravana was a learned and pious man, wise, just and peaceful ruler, a loving husban a fond father and brother, and a famo lutist and composer. "The readers of th *Ramayana*" so wrote a discerning critic an a famous historical scholar, "are familiar wi the austere penance he performed for a gre length of time, accompanied with such sel sacrifice as was unknown to Aryans. (Arany kanda, C. 32 and Uttarakanda, C. 10). Th was at the beginning of his career, but hi subsequent life shows that he allowed not single day to pass without worshipping th Sivalinga with choicest flowers and sanda (Uttara. 36). His piety is also exemplified b the innumerable hymns he sang, set to music in honour of Siva on the Kailas (*Ibid.*, C. 16) He was also versed in the foreign lore of th Vedas, Angas, and Sastras (Aranyakanda C. 32). In addition to music he was also a patron of the other fine arts, as will be seen from the fact that they had attained perfection in his dominions. Certainly the character of the individual who fosters these cannot be depraved". As a ruler, he made expeditions of conquest beyond the confines of his king- dom, but there were no internal dissensions or internecine wars. With his brother Dravidian monarchs he lived in peace and amity. (Uttara. 37, 39). He loved his brother Kumba-Karna, pictured as a huge gormandizer, so well that no thought of desertion ever crossed his mind in times of utmost crisis. He was true to his brother and said,

> "Joy thee in thy pleasures, Ravan, rule thy realm in regal pride,
> When I slay the hermit Rama, widowed Sita be thy bride!"

In the Introduction to Book IX, entitled Ravana Sabha, R. C. Dutt writes: "It is noticeable that Ravana's second brother, Kumba-Karna, also had the courage to censure his elder's action. But unlike Bibishan he was determined to fight for his king whether he was right or wrong. *There is a touch of sublimity in this devoted loyalty of Kumba-Karna* to the cause of his king and country".

Ravana's love for his sister, Surpanaka, was the cause of the Titanic War. He truly repented when he knew that he had unconsciously committed the sin of slaying his own brother-in-law and made ample amends for it by appointing her Vicerene over the Empire of Janasthanam. Though Mandothari, in her lamentation, called her 'Kodum-pāvi' or the greatest sinner, Ravana gave up his power and pelf, his realm and royalty, his life and pleasures, for her sake.

Ravana's conjugal love was none the less intense. It was his fortune that he had, in Mandothari, a typical woman and a darling wife. Pious and pure in life and blest with children, heroic and virtuous, she loved Ravana, and was ever his ministering angel and saviour.

Ravana's love for his sons was worthy of himself as a father. When the messenger cried that 'the light of Raksha valour was quenched', meaning thereby that Indrajit was slain by Lakshmana, the father's yearning heart was filled with anguish and his fleeting senses failed, and he wept and wailed.

"The monarch heard the mournful tale:
His heart was faint, his cheek was pale:
His fleeting sense at length regained,
In trembling tones he thus complained:
Ah me, my son, my pride; the boast
And glory of the giant host.
Could Lakshmana's puny might defeat
The foe whom Indra feared to meet?.....
And wast thou conquered by a boy?
I will not weep: thy noble deed

Has blessed thee with immortal meed
Gained by each hero in the skies
Who, fighting for his sovereign, dies......
But earth to me, with hill and plain,
Is desolate ; for thou art slain......
I fondly hoped thy hand should pay
Due honours on my dying day :
And couldst thou, O beloved, flee
And leave thy funeral rites to me ?
Life has no comfort left me, none,
O Indrajit, my son, my son." (Bk. VI, C. 93.)

Can any 'putraṣókam' transcend this in the intensity of its grief and sorrow ?

Considered on every side and viewed from all points, Ravana was supremely intelligent, erudite, mighty, discreet, and amiable, and he was a great and good man, 'one of the highest and noblest specimens of humanity'.

Why has the Aryan Chronicler painted him as a monster with ten heads and twenty arms and as a destroyer of human life ? The reason is not far to seek. The wife of ar Aryan prince was abducted. The sacrifices of the trespassing Aryan rishis were molested. The Dravidian hero is painted black here and there to set off the Aryan prince, the hero of the epic, as an ideal man and lover and a flawless and victorious prince. Valmiki, who has described the mock lamentation of tl Judas-like Vibishana who assumed the purp without loss of time and setting at naught tl law of primogeniture, which required a dire descendant of Ravana installed on the thron closes the epic with the Aryan's high esteer of his race and his supercilious contempt fo an aborigine as a rude barbarian.

> " And Ravan's death, by every tongue,
> And Rama's glorious deeds were sung....
> And Sita's truth which naught could bend "

He puts these words in the mouths of Vibishana and Rama respectively;

> " Nay one who scorned all sacred vows
> And dared to touch another's spouse,
> Fell tyrant of the human race,
> With funeral rites I may not grace ".
> " *Hatred dies*
> *When low in dust the foeman lies....*
> Let funeral rites be duly paid,
> *And be it mine thy toil to aid* ".

CHAPTER XI.

CONCLUSION.

Rama, the Kshatrya prince, came to be deified in process of time and he is looked upon and worshipped as an incarnation of Vishnu. The Rama-Nama is a tharaka mantram with hosts of Hindus. This belief forming the fundamental doctrine of the religious system of Ramanuja in the twelfth and of Ramananda in the fourteenth century, accounts for the wide prevalence and popularity of the Rama-Vishnu cult. In South India *The Four Thousand Hymns* by Alwars of different castes or classes have given it a fixity and a permanence which it could not have gained otherwise.

The Epic of Rama, Lassen held, "was intended to represent *allegorically* the first attempt of the Aryans to conquer the South. But Rama is nowhere described as founding an Aryan realm in the Dekhan, nor is any such intention on his part indicated anywhere in the epic. Weber subsequently expressed the same view in a somewhat modified form. According to him, the

Ramayana was meant to account for he spread of Aryan culture to the South and to Ceylon. But this form of the allegor al theory also lacks any confirmation from he statements of the epic itself; for Ran 's expedition is nowhere represented as pro u-cing any change or improvement in the civ li-zation of the South. The poet knows noth ig about the Dekhan beyond the fact t at Brahmin hermitages are to be found there".

According to Jacobi, the epic is based n Indian mythology. A celestial myth of the Veda has been transformed into a narrati e of earthly adventures. In the Rig-Veda S a appears as the furrow personified and invok d as a goddess. The Grihya Sutras represe t her as a genius of the ploughed field, prais d for her great beauty, and as the wife of Ind a or Parjanya, the rain-god. In the epic Si a emerges from the earth when her fath r Janaka turns a furrow. Rama is no oth than Indra, and his conflict with Ravana, tl Chief of the Rakshas, represents the Indr Vrita myth of the Rig-Veda. "This ident fication is confirmed by the name of Ravana son being Indrajit, 'Conqueror of Indra', c Indrasatru, 'Foe of Indra', the latter bein actually an epithet of Vritra in the Rig-Ved

Ravan's most notable feat, the rape of Sita, has its prototype in the stealing of the cows recovered by Indra. Hanumat(n), the chief of the monkeys and Rama's ally in the recovery of Sita, is the son of the wind-god, with the patronymic Maruti, and is described as flying hundreds of leagues through the air to find Sita. Hence in his figure perhaps survives a reminiscence of Indra's alliance with the Maruts in his conflict with Vrita, and of the dog Sarama who, as Indra's messenger, crosses the waters of the Rasa and tracks the cows. Sarama recurs in the name of a demoness who consoles Sita in her captivity".

Mr. R. C. Dutt* thus delivers himself on the historicity of the twin epics. "Like the Mahabaratha, the Ramayana is utterly valueless as a narrative of historical events and incidents. As in the Mahabaratha, so in the Ramayana, the heroes are myths pure and simple. . . . . Sita, the field furrow, had received divine honours from the time of the Rig-Veda, and had been worshipped as a goddess. When cultivation gradually spread in Southern India, it was not difficult to invent a political myth that Sita was carried to the

* Early Hindu Civilisation, Vol. I, p. 138.

South. And when she, as a goddess and woman—the noblest creation of human imagination—had acquired a distinct and lovely individuality, she was naturally described as the daughter of the holiest and most learned king on record, Janaka of the Videhas. . . . But who is Rama, described in the Epic as Sita's husband and the King of Kosalas? The later Puranas tell us that he was an incarnation of Vishnu, but *Vishnu himself had not risen to prominence at the time of which we are speaking.* Indra was still the Chief of the gods of the Epic period. And in the Sutra literature (*e.g.*, Paraskara Grihya Sutra II-17, 97, we learn that Sità, the furrow goddess, is the wife of Indra. Is it then an untenable conjecture that Rama, the hero of the Ramayana, is in his original conception, like Arjuna the hero of the Mahabaratha, only a new edition of Indra battling with the demons of drought. The myth of Indra has thus been mixed up with the Epic which describes an historic war in Northern India, and with the Epic which describes the historic conquest of Southern India".

In *The Dream of Ravan: A Mystery* by G. R. S. M., Ravana is represented as the Titanic, or in other words, the anti-Brahmnical, aboriginal fetish-worshipping monarch of Lanka or Ceylon...The hostile struggle with and death at the hands of Vishnu incarnate in the person of Rama, so far from being a punishment to the soul, was its triumph—was in fact, in union with the Deity, a more rapid and royal road for its attainment than the slow and wearisome path of devotion. Thus all Ravana's subsequent violence and crime receives a religious colouring. However, the slave of earthly passion to the eyes of men, his whole conduct was really motived upon this determination to bring on the beatific catastrophe and speed the collision which was to unite him with the Supreme Soul of the world;—an interpretation of action which, however startling, seems to flow as a necessary result from a pantheistic view of the universe........The ideal of happiness to the Hindu female is a perpetuity of renewed union with the one lord of her life. Mandothari's virtues and fidelity render it worthy of a vindicator, and a perpetual theodice is a part of their very office....Mandothari (signifying weighty stomach) was the virtuous Titaness and a very corpulent lady....The disinterested affection and elevated spiritualism of the dusky queen are noteworthy....The Titanic nature partakes largely of the Rajas and, i lesser measure, of the satvic quality."

The allegorical, mythical, and spiritu interpretations of the Epic of Rama do nc affect the historical character of Ravana. Th Aryans might have found his prototype i Indra, a nature-god, but the Dravidians hav looked upon him as a mighty hero anc monarch, a conqueror of worlds, and a fearles resister of the Aryan aggressions in South India. So great an admiration did he command that St. Jnana Sambandar, the celebrated Dravida Sisu, in his hymn in praise of the holy ashes, says 'இராவணன் மேலதும் நீறு' *i.e.*, the holy ashes were upon (worn by) even Ravana, the most powerful and dreaded sovereign of the ancient time. No higher eulogy can be thought of for any son of man. In the words of Macbeth *mutatis mutandis*, Ravana might say,

> " I dared do all that did become a man,
> Who dares do more, is none"—
>
> Macbeth I, Sc. vii.

APPENDIX.

LANKA.

From the Sketches of Ceylon History by the Hon'ble P. Arunachalam, M. A., Cantab :—

The Arabs called Ceylon Serendib and the Portuguese Ceilao. To the inhabitants of the neighbouring continent of India it was known centuries before the Christian era by the name of Lanka (the resplendent), the name it still bears among the native inhabitants, both Sinhalese and Tamil. The Siamese have added the honorific Tewa, calling the island Tewa Lanka, 'divine Lanka'. To the Chinese Ceylon was "the island of jewels", to the Greeks 'the land of the hyacinth and the ruby', to the Indian Buddhist 'the pearl upon the brow of India'.

The geology and fauna of the island point clearly to a time when Ceylon was part of an oriental continent, which stretched in unbroken land from Madagascar to the Malay Archipelago and northwards to the present valley of the Ganges. The valley was then occupied by a sea spreading westward across Persia, Arabia, and the Sahara Desert, and forming the southern limit of the

Palæ-arctic continent, which embraced Europe, North Africa and North Asia. In the course of ages the greater part of the oriental continent was submerged in the sea, leaving Ceylon as a fragment in the centre with, on one side, the Maldives, Laccadives, Seychelles, Mauritius, and Madagascar, themselves separated from one another by hundreds of miles of sea, and, on the other, the Malay Islands; while the Ganges valley was upheaved, making North and South India one land, and, later, Ceylon itself was separated from South India by a narrow sea.

Lanka the Resplendent earned this name on account of the glimmering of the rubies and gems on her surface. Ilankai is synonymous with the Tamil *trutti* and *arankam* (a rising ground or dry glimmering spot in a river, an ait or islet). Ilankai comes from the Tamil verb *ilanku-kiratu*—to shine or glimmer and means 'that which glimmers', a fit name for an ait in the midst of a shining sheet of water.

"The Cingalese traditions mention that thousands of isles attached to the kingdom of Lanka were overwhelmed by the sea B. C. 2387, along with the splendid capital of Sri Lankapoora which stood to the westward of the present island*......If there is any truth in the Ramayana or the 'Ravana Katawa' of Ceylon, the Maldives and Laccadives were then parts of the kingdom of Ravana, and, along with the great extent of Lanka, which was submerged, and the Southern Peninsula of India, formed the kingdom over which he ruled" (Major Forbes).

"The change of Ilanka into Lanka needs little explanation. The spirit of the Aryan languages where, unlike in the Tamil, the letter *L* can begin a word, would naturally eliminate the intitial I in assimilating the name into its vocabulary".

The meridian of Lanka of the Indian astronomers, which was reputed to pass through Ravana's capital, passes through the Maldive islands at 75° 53′ 15″ East Greenwich, quite four hundred miles from the present western limit of Ceylon. The Great Basses Lighthouse, which stands out on a solitary rock in the south-east sea of Ceylon, is still called Ravana's fort.

Sita's name lives in Ceylon in Sitatalawa (Sita's plain) and Sita-Ela (Sita's

* A second commotion is ascribed to the age of Panduvasa B.C. 504, and the subsidence of the shore adjacent to Colombo is said to have taken place 200 years later in the reign of Deventipiatissa, B. C. 306.—(Tennent).

stream) and Sita-kunt (Sita's pond) betwee Nuwara Eliya and Hakgala, where she is saic to have been confined by Ravana, and ir Sita-waka (Avissa-wella).

The earliest Indian tradition about Ceylon is recorded in the *Skanda Purāna*, the story of the rise and fall of a mighty and wicked Titan, for whose overthrow Skanda or Kartikeya, the god of war and wisdom, was incarnated. The echoes of that contest live in a remote forest shrine in the south-eastern corner of the island, called after him Kartikeya Grama, or Katagagama, where, after his victory, he wooed and won a chieftain's daughter, who shares with him the worship of millions from Cashmere to Ceylon, and with whom the Sinhalese priests (Kapuralas) of the shrine proudly claim kinship.

The first historical event recorded in the chronicles is the landing of Wijaya, the discarded scion of a royal race in Northern India and the founder of the first known dynasty in Ceylon. This event is assigned to the year 544 B. C.

In an article contributed to the *Oriental*, a magazine published in Calcutta, Kehel Paunala Pohath Mudaliyar writes as follows: 'My contention is that the statement in the Ceylon histories that the name *Sinhala* originated with Sinha Bahu, the father of King Wijaya, who landed in Lanka 543 B. C. is not correct, because the name *Sinhala* is mentioned in the Mahabharata which was composed *at least 700 years* before the landing of Wijaya in Ceylon. You will find the name *Sinhala* in Sabha Parva p. 49, Gangs of the *Sinhalas*, Chap. 52, v. 36. 'Chiefs of the *Sinhalas* and the aboriginal tribes of Lanka', and in Vana Parva, p. 76, Chap. 51, vv. 22-6.

"In ancient Tamil classics Sinhala is mentioned as one of the seventeen countries lying around Tamilaham or the home of the Tamils."

"Taprobane, Tampapanni (copper coloured) or Tamraparani (tamra varuna= copper water) so-called by some early Tamil settlers from Southern India who arrived in Ceylon and called it after the river in the Tinnevelly district."

'The contention that Tambapanni means the Red Land is supported by the Chinese name of Ceylon, *Suychoo*, which means the *red land*.'

Sir Emerson Tennent writes: 'A peculiarity which is one of the first to strike a stranger who lands at Galle or Colombo is the *bright red* colour of the streets and roads contrasting vividly with the verdure of the trees.

The name *Zeilan* occurs in Gene is, chap. viii of the Samaritan Pentateuch, he antiquity of which is referred to the reig of Rehoboam B. C. 975-958. Tarshish has be n, by European scholars identified with he modern Point de Galle in Ceylon.

The name *Ilam* is a pure Tamil name of this island of gems, on account of its re u-tation for *gold* or *toddy*. Megasthenes d s-cribes this island ' as being divided by a river into two sections, the one infested y wild beasts and elephants, and the other p o-ducing *gold* and gems.

Ceylon is also known to the Tamils s *Ponnagar* or golden city.

Thennai, Thenku, Thenna-maram— l mean tree of the *South*, and the Tamil expre -sion *Illattu Tenkay*, confirms this theor . There is a general belief among the India s that the Shanars of the Tinnevelly district a members of the Chandoo community Ceylon and that they were induced to imm grate to India, at the time of the introductio of the cocoanut palm by conferring on the chiefs such titles as *Nadars*, gramani, etc These Shanars have been known in India a *Ila-kulattu Shanar* (Shanar of the Ceylo tribe) as we read in the Peria Purana" (S. W Coomarasawmy).